KW-265-278

seafood

seafood

snacks, salads, soups and more

RYLAND
PETERS
& SMALL

LONDON NEW YORK

Designer Luana Gobbo

Editor Sharon Cochrane

Picture Research Emily Westlake

Production Paul Harding

Editorial Director Julia Charles

Art Director Anne-Marie Bulat

Publishing Director Alison Starling

First published in the United Kingdom in 2006
by Ryland Peters & Small
20–21 Jockey's Fields
London WC1R 4BW
www.rylandpeters.com

10 9 8 7 6 5 4 3 2 1

Text copyright © Julz Beresford, Vatcharin Bhumichitr,
Maxine Clark, Clare Ferguson, Manisha Gambhir
Harkins, Elsa Petersen-Schepelern, Linda Tubby and
Ryland Peters & Small 2006
Design and photographs copyright ©
Ryland Peters & Small 2006

The authors' moral rights have been asserted. All
rights reserved. No part of this publication may be
reproduced, stored in a retrieval system or transmitted in any
form or by any means, electronic, mechanical, photocopying
or otherwise, without the prior permission of the publisher.

ISBN-13: 978 1 84597 127 4
ISBN-10: 1 84597 127 2

A catalogue record for this book is available from
the British Library.

Printed in China

Notes
• All spoon measurements are level unless
otherwise specified.
• All eggs are medium unless otherwise
specified. Uncooked or partly cooked eggs
should not be served to the very young, the
very old, those with compromised immune
systems or to pregnant women.

LINCOLNSHIRE
COUNTY COUNCIL

contents

introduction **7**

snacks & starters **8**

salads **24**

soups **34**

mains **44**

pasta & rice **54**

index & credits **64**

introduction

Seafood is wonderfully versatile – it can be used in soups and salads, risottos and pasta dishes, salads and tarts and simply on its own. From Southeast Asia to the Mediterranean, seafood is used in many different and delicious ways.

Seafood is easy to prepare, so don't be afraid to cook it at home. Just ensure you follow a few simple guidelines. Always buy seafood from a reputable source and when it is as fresh as possible – choose whatever looks the freshest and best on the day. Store it in the refrigerator until required, and eat it preferably on the day of purchase. If you are using frozen seafood, ensure that it is thoroughly thawed in the refrigerator before cooking. Shellfish should be alive when you buy it fresh and uncooked. Check any open mussels or clams by tapping them against the work surface; they should close when you do so, discard any that stay open.

It is easy to overcook seafood, so watch it carefully while it is cooking and follow the timings in the recipes closely. If it is cooked too long, it will be tough.

Light, healthy and delicious, seafood is perfect for any occasion. Whether your passion is for scallops or squid, clams or crayfish, this international recipe collection is guaranteed to inspire you.

snacks & starters

This traditional tapas dish is perfect served with a cold beer. It is a simple recipe and can be whipped up in no time at all. This method of deep-frying will make the batter crisp, while the prawns remain tender and juicy inside. Cook them in small batches so as not to reduce the temperature of the oil.

300 g uncooked prawns, shell on

125 g plain flour

1 teaspoon baking powder

a pinch of salt

a pinch of oak-smoked sweet Spanish paprika

250 ml beer

oil, for deep-frying

lemon wedges, to serve

an electric deep-fryer

SERVES 4

prawns in overcoats

Peel the prawns, but leave the tail fins intact. Sieve the flour, baking powder, salt and paprika into a bowl, mix well, then gently stir in the beer. Let rest for a few minutes.

Fill a deep-fryer with oil to the manufacturer's recommended level and heat the oil to 195°C (380°F). Dip the prawns in the batter, then fry in the hot oil, in small batches, until golden brown. Remove from the oil, drain on kitchen paper and keep them warm while you fry the remaining batches. Serve hot with wedges of lemon.

spicy crab in filo cups

9 sheets of filo pastry, about A4 paper size

50 g butter, melted

Spicy crab filling

200 g canned white crab meat in brine, drained

75 g canned water chestnuts, drained and finely chopped or sliced

3 cm piece of fresh ginger, peeled and cut into thin strips

2 spring onions, trimmed and thinly sliced

finely grated zest and juice of 1 unwaxed lime

1 garlic clove, crushed

½ fresh red chilli, deseeded and finely chopped

2 teaspoons sesame oil

2 tablespoons chopped fresh coriander

sea salt and freshly ground black pepper

3 mini muffin tins, 12 holes each, brushed with melted butter

MAKES ABOUT 36

These delicate bites are as light as air, but packed with fresh Asian flavours. Use canned white crab meat from the Pacific for these – not only does it taste very good, but there is no shell or messy bits to deal with if you are catering for a large number of people. It is also much cheaper than fresh crab.

Unroll the filo and cut the stack into 108 squares, each measuring 7 x 7 cm. To do this, keep the sheets stacked on top of each other, then mark the top sheet into 12 squares. Cut down through all the layers, giving 108 squares. Pile into 2–3 stacks and keep beside you in a plastic bag.

To make a filo cup, take 3 squares of filo, brush each with melted butter and lay one on top of the other, so that the points of the 3 squares overlap to make a star, and do not touch each other. Quickly but gently press into one of the holes of the prepared muffin tin, so the points of the filo shoot upwards like a handkerchief. Repeat with all the remaining filo until you have 36 cups.

Bake in a preheated oven at 180°C (350°F) Gas 4 for 8–10 minutes until golden. Remove from the oven, let cool in the tin, then carefully remove to a tray (they are very fragile).

Put the crab in a bowl and fluff up with a fork. Stir in the water chestnuts, ginger and spring onions. In a separate bowl, mix the lime zest and juice, crushed garlic, chilli and sesame oil. Season to taste with salt and pepper. Mix this into the crab mixture (this can be done up to 4 hours in advance), then stir in the chopped coriander.

Fill the cups with the crab mixture just before serving (they can go a little soggy if they are kept too long).

The contrast of the golden crunchy breadcrumbs and the soft mussel meat is fantastic. Cooking mussels in this way is typically Italian and really delicious. Although this recipe may seem a lot of work, it is well worth it.

baked mussels
with crispy breadcrumbs

1.5 kg fresh mussels, in the shell

150 ml white wine

2 garlic cloves, lightly crushed

3 tablespoons olive oil, plus extra for sprinkling

1 onion, very finely chopped

150 g stale but not dried breadcrumbs

4 tablespoons finely chopped fresh flat leaf parsley

freshly squeezed juice of 1 lemon

sea salt and freshly ground black pepper

a large baking dish or 4 individual baking dishes

a baking sheet

SERVES 4

Scrub and debeard the mussels. Tap them all against the work surface and discard any that don't close – they are dead – and any with damaged shells.

Put the mussels in a large saucepan, add the wine and garlic, cover tightly with a lid and cook over high heat for 4–5 minutes until they just start to open. Discard any that do not open. Strain through a colander and reserve the juices.

When the mussels have cooled, twist off all the empty half-shells and arrange the mussels in a single layer in a large baking dish or individual baking dishes set on a baking sheet.

Heat the olive oil in a frying pan, add the onion and fry for about 5 minutes until soft. Reduce the heat, add the breadcrumbs and parsley and stir well so that all the breadcrumbs absorb the oil. Cook for a further 5 minutes to brown the breadcrumbs a little.

Sprinkle this mixture over the mussels, trickle over the extra olive oil and the lemon juice and bake in a preheated oven at 220°C (425°F) Gas 7 for 5 minutes. Reheat the strained mussel liquid in a saucepan, add salt and pepper to taste (take care because it may already be salty), then pour around the mussels before serving, if liked.

spanish clams
with ham

500 g fresh clams, in the shell or frozen raw clams

2 tablespoons extra virgin olive oil

50 g jamón serrano or Parma ham, cut into thin strips

1 small green chilli, deseeded and chopped

2 garlic cloves, sliced

4 tablespoons white wine or cider

2 tablespoons chopped spring onion tops, chives or parsley

SERVES 4

Mediterranean live clams usually go straight into the cooking pot, with oil and garlic. Herbs and a splash of wine are sometimes added. However, because Spanish cured hams are so exceptional, adding even a little will season and enliven many such savoury dishes. Mar i montaña (sea and mountain) is a typically Catalan cooking idea which has spread worldwide.

If using live clams, tap them against the work surface and discard any that don't close – they are dead – and any with damaged shells. Put the clams (fresh or frozen), olive oil, ham, chilli and garlic in a flameproof casserole and stir over high heat. When the ham is cooked and the clams begin to open, add the wine or cider, cover the pan and tilt it several times to mix the ingredients. Cook over high heat for a further 2–3 minutes or until all the clams have opened and are cooked (discard any that do not open).

Sprinkle with chopped spring onions, chives or parsley. Cover and cook for 1 minute more, then ladle into shallow soup bowls and serve immediately.

sizzled scallops with lemon

Scallops are a popular seafood in Italy. Try to buy fresh scallops in the shell and get your fishmonger to open, clean and trim them for you. Allow three or four scallops per person, depending on their size, your appetite and budget. If using frozen scallops, they must be fully thawed, patted dry and cooked more carefully, because they absorb a lot of water and create more steam.

Put 1 teaspoon of the lemon zest in a bowl, add the sea salt and garlic and mix gently.

Pat the scallops dry with kitchen paper and add to the bowl.

Heat a non-stick frying pan, add the butter and oil and heat until sizzling. Add the scallops and cook for 1–1½ minutes on each side or until golden. The inside should be barely heated through, barely cooked, silky smooth and opaque.

Reduce the heat and add the lemon juice and wine or vermouth to the pan. Push the scallops to one side and tilt the pan to pool the juices. Add the mascarpone or cream cheese, if using, and stir it into the sauce. Heat until the sauce thickens slightly and evaporates to a creamy glaze.

Serve the scallops inside the deep shells or on small plates with the sauce spooned over. Sprinkle with some freshly ground black pepper and accompany by slices of lemon and toasted ciabatta.

finely grated zest and freshly squeezed juice of 1 unwaxed lemon

1 teaspoon sea salt flakes, crushed

2 garlic cloves, crushed

12–16 prepared scallops, and their deep shells if available

50 g butter

2 tablespoons extra virgin olive oil

2 tablespoons white wine or vermouth

2 tablespoons mascarpone or cream cheese, cut into small pieces (optional)

freshly ground black pepper

To serve

1 lemon, halved and sliced

sliced ciabatta bread, toasted

SERVES 4–6

squid with mayonnaise

Cuttlefish or squid, either whole tiny ones or larger ones sliced into rings, are favourites all around the Mediterranean, and in good bars and restaurants worldwide. In Spain, they are dipped in flour and sizzled until crisp, often accompanied by a stinging, garlicky mayonnaise called alioli.

about 150 g semolina flour

1 teaspoon sea salt

1 teaspoon dried oregano or marjoram leaves, crumbled

8 medium squid or cuttlefish tubes, sliced into 1 cm rounds

virgin olive oil, for deep-frying

2 lemons, halved, to serve

Alioli

6–8 fat garlic cloves, crushed

½ teaspoon sea salt

100 ml extra virgin olive oil

an electric deep-fryer

SERVES 4

Put the semolina flour, salt and oregano or marjoram in a bowl. Pat the squid rings dry with kitchen paper and toss them in the flour mixture until well coated. Set them aside, not touching each other, while you make the sauce.

To make the alioli, put the garlic and salt in a mortar and crush to a sticky paste with a pestle. Pour in the oil in a fine stream, beating or whisking constantly in one direction until creamy. Continue adding the oil and mixing to form a thick, glossy emulsion. Alternatively, use a bowl and a hand-held electric mixer.

Fill a deep-fryer with the oil to the manufacturer's recommended level and heat to 190°C (375°F). Fry the prepared squid or cuttlefish in the hot oil in batches of about 8. Cook for 30–45 seconds, the minimum time it takes to set the seafood to firm whiteness and make the coating crisp. Remove from the oil, drain on kitchen paper and keep hot. Continue frying the squid in batches until all are cooked.

Serve a pile of squid rings on each of 4 plates, with ½ lemon for squeezing, and a large spoonful of the alioli beside or in bowls.

Variation Provençal aïoli, another version of alioli, can be made in a food processor, but the quantities must be larger to let the blades run. Put the garlic and salt from the main recipe in a food processor, add 2 egg yolks and 1 whole egg, and blend until creamy. Gradually pour in about 220 ml olive oil until the mixture is thick and emulsified. You will find it becomes very thick. Blend in 1–2 tablespoons freshly squeezed lemon juice at the end. This quantity will serve 8 (more than the main recipe). If making ahead of time, cover closely with clingfilm and store in the refrigerator for up to 3 days.

Calamaretti (baby squid) are a favourite in Italy, especially in seaside trattorias. If your fishmonger doesn't sell fresh baby squid, he will almost certainly have fresh or frozen prepared squid bodies. Buy the smallest you can find, stuff them loosely and cook for a few minutes more until firm and densely white. You will miss out on the crispy tentacles and the flavourful pink skins, but the dish will still taste good.

stuffed oven-roasted baby squid

500 g whole baby squid, fresh or frozen and thawed

½ teaspoon sea salt flakes, crushed

¼ teaspoon dried chilli flakes or crushed black peppercorns

4–6 tablespoons extra virgin olive oil

Herb stuffing

2 tablespoons chopped fresh marjoram, oregano or dill

4 tablespoons chopped fresh flat leaf parsley

2 slices of *prosciutto cotto* or cooked ham, chopped

2 teaspoons grated unwaxed lemon zest

2 slices of stale white bread, crumbled, about 75 g

wooden cocktail sticks

SERVES 4–6

To make the stuffing, put the herbs, prosciutto or ham, lemon zest and bread in a food processor and chop in a series of brief pulses. The mixture should be coarse.

To prepare the squid, wash it, then drain and pat dry with kitchen paper. Pull the tentacles out of the bodies. Trim off and discard the eyes and tiny beak in the middle of the star of tentacles. Rinse out the contents of the body and discard the transparent quill. Some people remove the pinky mauve skin, but you can leave it as it adds flavour and colour.

Loosely pack the stuffing mixture inside the squid bodies and close the ends with a wooden cocktail stick. Dust the stuffed squid and the tentacles with the salt and chilli flakes or pepper. Arrange them in a shallow roasting tin.

Put the olive oil in a saucepan and heat until hot. Pour over the squid and roast towards the top of a preheated oven at 200°C (400°F) Gas 6 for 5–8 minutes or until the flesh sets white and firm and the stuffing smells aromatic. Serve hot or warm.

marinated octopus

Some people avoid cooking octopus because they think it can be tough. In Spain, octopus are banged against the jetty by the fishermen to make them tender. If you don't have a fisherman on hand, tap the octopus with a meat mallet, or buy them frozen (freezing also helps tenderize them). Then you should cook them long and slow at a low temperature. Octopus keeps well, and the longer you marinate it, the better the flavour.

If the octopus hasn't been frozen or tenderized in any way, you should bang it against a hard surface 10 times or more.

Bring a large saucepan of water to the boil, then add the octopus and blanch it for 30 seconds at a time, repeating 4–5 times. Return the octopus to the saucepan, cover with a lid and simmer for 1 hour.

Test the octopus for tenderness – if it's still tough, continue cooking for another 20 minutes. Remove from the heat, let cool, then drain. Cut the tentacles into 2 cm lengths and the bodies into bite-sized pieces.

Heat the oil in a frying pan, add the vinegar, garlic, 2 tablespoons of the parsley, the paprika, chilli flakes, capers and octopus. Bring to the boil, then simmer for 3 minutes. Transfer to a plastic or ceramic dish, let cool, season with salt and pepper, then let marinate in the refrigerator overnight.

Serve at room temperature with the lemon juice and the remaining parsley sprinkled over the top.

4 baby octopus, about 500 g, cleaned (see Note page 30)

3 tablespoons fruity olive oil

2 tablespoons red wine vinegar

2 garlic cloves, crushed

3 tablespoons chopped fresh flat leaf parsley

½ teaspoon oak-smoked sweet Spanish paprika

½ teaspoon dried chilli flakes

1 tablespoon capers, chopped

freshly squeezed juice of 1 lemon

sea salt and freshly ground black pepper

SERVES 4

salads

This way of cooking mussels, based on the traditional recipe of mussels in white wine and garlic, makes a perfect summer salad.

mussels in ice wine

2 kg large fresh mussels, in the shell

250 ml fruity white wine, such as Chardonnay

3 garlic cloves, crushed

1 small onion, chopped

a sprig of fresh thyme

1 bay leaf

2 sprigs of fresh parsley

a small bunch of chives, scissor-snipped

ice cubes, to serve

SERVES 4–6

Scrub and debeard the mussels. Tap them all against the work surface and discard any that don't close – they are dead – and any with damaged shells.

Put a layer of ice cubes in a small roasting dish and put a wire rack on top.

Put the wine, garlic, onion, thyme, bay leaf and parsley in a large saucepan and bring to the boil. Working in batches, add the prepared mussels, put on the lid and let steam until they open, 1–2 minutes. Remove the mussels from the pan with a straining spoon as they open. Discard any that don't open. Take the empty shell off the top and put the mussel in its bottom shell on the rack over ice. Repeat with the remaining batches of mussels.

When the mussels are cool, cover with clingfilm and keep in the refrigerator until ready to serve. Check from time to time that the melted ice isn't flooding them – pour it off if it does, so the water doesn't dilute the mussel flavour.

Strain the cooking liquid. It may be gritty, so strain through muslin if necessary. Let cool, then chill in the refrigerator.

Put a serving platter in the freezer. When ready to serve, spread a layer of ice cubes on the platter and arrange the mussels on top. Sprinkle with some snipped chives, then spoon the cooking liquid over the top – you need a little in each shell.

spicy thai prawn salad

1 tablespoon peanut oil

1 tablespoon Thai red curry paste

12 uncooked prawns, shelled, deveined and halved lengthways

12 cherry tomatoes, halved

a handful of fresh mint sprigs, to serve

Spicy Thai dressing

1 stalk of lemongrass, outer leaves discarded, remainder very finely chopped

2 fresh red bird's eye chillies, thinly sliced and deseeded, if preferred

2 Thai pink shallots or 1 small regular shallot, thinly sliced lengthways

1 tablespoon brown sugar or palm sugar

freshly squeezed juice of 2 limes

grated zest of 2 kaffir limes

a handful of fresh coriander leaves, finely chopped

3 spring onions, finely chopped

2 kaffir lime leaves, mid-rib removed, the leaves very thinly sliced crossways, then finely chopped

SERVES 4

This salad is very simple – you can also make it with pre-cooked prawns. Cutting the prawns in half lengthways makes them easier to eat and also makes them curl into pretty corkscrews when they are stir-fried. When preparing the lemongrass and kaffir lime leaves, make sure to slice them very thinly indeed. If you can't find them, use a squeeze of lemon juice and some grated regular lime zest instead. The grated zest of kaffir limes is much more scented and delicious than that of regular limes, which can be used if you can't find the real thing. Kaffir is a Hindi word meaning 'foreign', so throughout history people have thought these limes looked a little unusual.

Heat the oil and curry paste in a wok, add the prawns and stir-fry for about 1 minute until opaque. Let cool.

To make the dressing, crush the lemongrass, 1 chilli and half the shallots with a mortar and pestle. Add the sugar, lime juice and zest and mix well until the sugar dissolves. Stir in the remaining chilli and shallots, the coriander, spring onions and lime leaves.

Put the prawns in a serving bowl, add the cherry tomatoes, pour the dressing over the top and toss well. Serve, topped with mint sprigs.

Variations

• This dressing is also good with crab claws, either stir-fried or boiled.

• Use scallops instead of prawns. Prick the corals with a toothpick before cooking or they will explode in the heat.

• Try other Thai curry pastes, or a mixture of peanut oil and toasted sesame oil.

August is crayfish season in Sweden, when the shops are full of special crayfish party paraphernalia, such as paper hats, paper lanterns with sunny faces and candles for the table. Crayfish are traditional, but the dish is equally good made with large prawns.

swedish crayfish party

2 tablespoons sea salt

3 tablespoons dill seed

a large bunch of fresh dill, tied up with string

10–20 uncooked crayfish or Dublin Bay prawns per person

To serve

a small bunch of fresh dill, preferably with flower heads

toast or crusty bread

unsalted butter

iced aquavit or vodka

beer

mayonnaise (optional)

SERVES 4–6

To cook the crayfish, start the day before. Put the salt, dill seed and bundle of dill in a large saucepan, add 2.5 litres water and bring to a rolling boil. Add the crayfish to the boiling water 5–6 at a time. Cover with a lid and simmer for about 5 minutes, or just until they turn red. Like all seafood, they shouldn't be cooked too long or they will be tough.

Remove the crayfish with a slotted spoon and transfer to a large bowl. Tuck more fresh dill between them. When all the crayfish are cooked, put the saucepan in a sink of cold water to bring down the temperature quickly. When a little cooler, strain the liquid over the crayfish and let cool completely. Keep in the refrigerator overnight or up to 24 hours.

If using ready-cooked crayfish or prawns, put them in a bowl with some fresh dill. Boil the water with the salt, dill seed and bunch of dill, let cool, then strain the liquid over the crayfish and chill as before.

When ready to serve, drain the crayfish and pile generously onto a large serving platter. Top with the bunch of dill and serve with toast or crusty bread, lots of good butter for spreading, aquavit or vodka and beer. Provide lobster crackers and picks, big napkins and finger bowls.

To eat the crayfish, remove its claws and crack them. Eat the meat with your fingers. Pull off the tail and cut it down the side. Pull out the tail meat and remove and discard the dark thread. Eat on buttered toast or bread – or all alone. You could serve the crayfish with a bowl of mayonnaise for dipping, if you like, but it's not traditional.

greek octopus salad

Greeks are in love with octopus and squid. This salad, with its deliciously fresh flavours, is guaranteed to transport you to the sunny islands of Greece. If you have a Greek fishmonger, ask him to remove the beak, eyes and insides of the octopus for you. If not, it is very easy to do this yourself (see note, below).

If the octopus hasn't been frozen or tenderized in any way, bang it against a hard surface 10 times or more.

Bring a large saucepan of water to the boil, add the garlic, oregano and dill and return to the boil. Add the octopus and blanch it for 30 seconds at a time, repeating 4–5 times. Return the octopus to the saucepan, cover with a lid, reduce the heat and simmer for 1 hour. Test the octopus for tenderness – if it's still tough, continue cooking for another 20 minutes.

Remove from the heat, let cool, then drain. Cut the octopus into bite-sized pieces.

Put all the dressing ingredients in a large bowl and beat with a fork. Add the octopus and toss to coat. Chill until you are ready to serve. Serve the octopus topped with sprigs of basil and dill and some chopped parsley.

*Notes

• To clean a large octopus, turn it upside down so the tentacles form a star. In the middle of the star is the hard beak. Cut it out and discard it. Make a slit down the body and rinse it out. Remove and discard the transparent quill.

• If you don't want to cook the octopus whole, prepare it like a squid. Pull off the tentacles – the insides should come out too. Cut the tentacles off just above their join, so they make a star. Cut out the beak as before. Rinse out the body. Keep the tentacles and body and discard the rest.

1–2 octopus (1–2 kg in total), cleaned*

3 garlic cloves, crushed

a sprig of fresh oregano

2–3 sprigs of fresh dill

Green herb dressing

5–6 tablespoons extra virgin olive oil

freshly squeezed juice of ½–1 lemon

a handful of fresh basil leaves, thinly sliced

leaves from a sprig of fresh oregano, chopped

1 tablespoon chopped fresh dill

sea salt and freshly ground black pepper

To serve

sprigs of fresh basil

sprigs of fresh dill

2 tablespoons chopped fresh parsley

SERVES 8–10

char-grilled scallop salad

It is important not to overcook scallops: cook them only until they become opaque (the time depends on their size). When you buy them, they should be creamy coloured. If they are white, they have been left to soak in water – they sponge up about 30 per cent of their own weight given half a chance – as soon as they hit the pan they drop it all and look limp and flaccid. You've paid good money for water! Serve this warm salad with a dry white wine.

250 g shelled green peas or broad beans

green salad leaves

8 very thin slices of smoked pancetta or streaky bacon

about 20 shelled scallops

4 tablespoons extra virgin olive oil

4 teaspoons white rice vinegar

sea salt and freshly ground black pepper

SERVES 4

Microwave the green peas or broad beans on HIGH for 2 minutes. Cool under running water, then transfer to a bowl of ice cubes and water. If using broad beans, pop them out of their grey skins, discard the skins and reserve the beans.

Arrange the salad leaves on 4 plates.

Heat a stove-top grill pan or non-stick frying pan, add the pancetta and cook until crisp and brown on both sides. Drain on kitchen paper. Add the scallops to the pan and cook over high heat for about 1 minute on each side until browned on the outside and opaque all the way through. If not, continue cooking for about 1 minute more, or until opaque. Do not overcook or the scallops will shrink and be tough.

Drain the peas or beans and divide them and the bacon among the plates. As soon as the scallops are cooked, add about 5 to each plate. Serve immediately, sprinkled with olive oil, vinegar, salt and pepper.

soups

Although Westerners like to have soup as a separate course, in Thailand it is served with other dishes. People ladle spoonfuls of soup from a communal bowl onto the rice on their plates. This soup, known as Tom Yam Kung, *is a traditional Thai recipe, with an aroma created by kaffir lime leaves and lemongrass. It is a must on the menu in all Thai restaurants, and easy to make at home.*

hot and sour soup
with prawns

1.25 litres chicken stock

1 tablespoon tom yam sauce*

4 kaffir lime leaves, finely chopped

2 stalks of tender lemongrass, coarsely sliced

3 tablespoons freshly squeezed lemon or lime juice

3 tablespoons Thai fish sauce

2 small fresh red or green chillies, thinly sliced

2 teaspoons sugar

12 straw mushrooms, halved (canned mushrooms will do)

12 uncooked king prawns, shelled, but with tail fins intact, and deveined

SERVES 4

Heat the stock in a saucepan and add the tom yam sauce. Stir in the lime leaves, lemongrass, lemon or lime juice, fish sauce, chillies and sugar. Bring to the boil and simmer for 2 minutes. Add the mushrooms and prawns, stir and cook for a further 2–3 minutes, or until the prawns are cooked through. Ladle into soup bowls and serve.

*Note Tom yam sauce is widely available, even in some supermarkets. If you can't find it, try an Oriental market.

laksa lemak

500 g uncooked prawns, shelled

2 tablespoons peanut oil

1.5 litres chicken stock

1 stalk of lemongrass, halved

2 kaffir lime leaves

2 sprigs of fresh lemon balm

4 thin slices of fresh ginger

1 teaspoon light soy sauce

400 ml canned coconut milk

125 g beansprouts

brown sugar, to taste

a bunch of coriander, chopped

sea salt

Laksa spice paste

a tiny piece of shrimp paste

4 red chillies, deseeded

1 stalk of lemongrass

6 shallots, coarsely chopped

1 teaspoon ground turmeric

1 garlic clove, chopped

½ teaspoon ground ginger

6 macadamia nuts

2 tablespoons Thai fish sauce

To serve

250 g thick Chinese egg noodles, freshly cooked and drained

10 cm cucumber, very thinly sliced

a handful of Chinese cabbage or Napa cabbage, shredded

SERVES 4–6

Laksa, the spicy prawn and noodle soup from Malaysia and Singapore, has become fashionable all over the world. This one is a speciality of the Nonya or Straits-Chinese community. Its bright yellow colour comes from turmeric and, on its home ground, fresh turmeric is often used rather than the ground turmeric found in the West.

To make the laksa spice paste, toast the shrimp paste in a dry frying pan or hot oven, then transfer to a blender. Chop the chillies finely. Discard the outer leaves of the lemongrass and chop the remainder very finely. Add the chillies and lemongrass to the blender along with all the other spice paste ingredients. Grind to a thick, chunky paste. You may need to add a little water to let the blades run. Alternatively, grind the ingredients with a mortar and pestle.

Remove the black veins from the prawns and set aside.

Heat the oil in a large saucepan and add the laksa paste. Sauté for about 8 minutes. Add the chicken stock, lemongrass, lime leaves, lemon balm, ginger and soy sauce. Bring to the boil and add the coconut milk, stirring to keep it from separating. Reduce the heat and simmer gently for 15 minutes.

Add the prawns, beansprouts, sugar and salt. Simmer for 2–3 minutes until the prawns are just cooked. Discard the lemon balm and lemongrass and add the chopped coriander.

To serve, put the noodles, cucumber and Chinese cabbage in 4 large or 6 smaller bowls, then ladle in the soup.

Note If you have the time, leave the broth, minus the prawns, for at least 1 hour for the flavours to mingle and mellow. Add the prawns just before you are ready to serve. Do not use ready-cooked prawns: their tough texture will spoil the dish.

thai lobster noodle soup

Like so much Thai food, this recipe has a delicate balance of spicy, fresh, zesty flavours. Kaffir lime leaves are now widely available, either as part of a Thai flavour pack in supermarkets, or in big bags from Asian or Chinatown markets. Buy the whole bag and freeze them, then use straight from frozen. Ginger can also be frozen, then grated from frozen. Both flavours contrast well with the richness of coconut milk and lobster. Seaweed and sesame seeds aren't traditional – less Thai than Japanese, but no less delicious for all that.

Put the lobster or crayfish shells, dried shrimp and kaffir lime leaves in a large saucepan. Add 1.5 litres water and bring to the boil, then lower the heat and simmer for 1 hour. Strain the stock, grate the ginger and squeeze the juice from it into the stock.

Soak the noodles in a bowl of cold water for 20 minutes. When soft, drain well and cover until needed. Put the seaweed in a bowl and stir in the mirin.

Add the coconut cream to the stock, stir well and bring to the boil. Lower the heat, then add fish sauce and lime juice to taste.

When ready to serve, add the drained noodles to the stock and reheat. Ladle into hot bowls, then add the chillies, chives, beans and lobster or crayfish meat. Drain the seaweed and sprinkle it over the soup, then top with Thai sweet basil leaves and serve.

Note Fishmongers and Chinese supermarkets often have frozen crayfish tails, which are good for this recipe. Instead of hijiki seaweed, you could sprinkle some black sesame seeds on top.

2 small cooked lobsters or crayfish tails, shells removed and reserved

120 g dried shrimp

3 kaffir lime leaves, torn

3 cm piece of fresh ginger, peeled

200 g wide rice noodles (*sen lek*)

2 tablespoons hijiki seaweed

2 tablespoons mirin (sweetened Japanese rice wine)

200 ml coconut cream

2 tablespoons Thai fish sauce

freshly squeezed juice of 1 lime

2 fresh mild red chillies, halved lengthways, deseeded and thinly sliced

2 fresh mild green chillies, halved lengthways, deseeded and thinly sliced

a handful of garlic chives, sliced diagonally

75 g thin green beans, halved lengthways and cooked

2 sprigs of fresh Thai sweet basil leaves (optional)

SERVES 4

There are many kinds of chowder – this New England variety, made with clams and cream; the Manhattan kind, made with tomatoes and clams; and the British kind, made with corn and smoked haddock instead of the clams.

clam chowder

2 kg fresh quahog clams, in the shell

125 ml fish stock or clam juice, plus extra fish stock to make 1 litre

500 g smoked pancetta, cut into cubes

sunflower oil (optional)

3 onions, coarsely chopped

1 celery stalk, chopped

1 carrot, chopped

2 bay leaves

a few sprigs of fresh thyme

250 g salad potatoes, peeled and cut into cubes

500 ml double cream

sea salt and freshly cracked black pepper

To serve

a large bunch of flat leaf parsley, coarsely chopped

crackers

SERVES 4

Put the clams in a large saucepan with 125 ml water and the fish stock or clam juice. Cover the pan, bring to the boil and boil hard for a few minutes until the clams open. Remove them as soon as they do and shell over a bowl. Don't overcook them or they will be tough. Discard the shells, reserve the clams and return the juice in the bowl to the pan. (Discard any clams that have not opened.) Strain the cooking liquid through a sieve, then through muslin into a measuring jug. Add enough fish stock to make up to 1 litre. Set aside.

Clean the pan, add the pancetta and cook over low heat to render the fat (add a dash of sunflower oil to encourage it if you like). Remove the crisp pancetta and set aside.

Add the onions, celery, carrot, bay leaves and thyme to the saucepan. Cook gently until the onions are softened and translucent. Add the potato cubes and the reserved 1 litre stock and simmer until the potatoes are done, about 10 minutes.

Chop half the clams, and cut the remainder in half through their thickness. Add the clams, pancetta and cream to the saucepan and heat through. Taste and add salt if necessary (remember the clam juices and pancetta are already salty). Remove and discard the bay leaves and thyme.

Ladle into warm soup bowls and serve sprinkled with lots of cracked pepper, crisp pancetta, handfuls of parsley and crackers on the side.

bouillabaisse

750 g fresh mussels, in the shell

4 tablespoons extra virgin olive oil

4 garlic cloves, crushed

500 ml dry white wine

1 small bunch of flat leaf parsley

1 small bunch of thyme

a pinch of cayenne

1.25 litres water or fish stock

a large pinch of saffron threads

1 head fennel, sliced lengthways

4 large ripe tomatoes, cubed

2 kg assorted prepared white fish: such as cod, snapper, gurnard, mullet, monkfish, bream or conger eel, cut into 5 cm chunks

350 g prepared baby squid (see page 21), sliced or whole

2 tablespoons Pernod or Ricard, to taste (optional)

sea salt flakes

Croûtes

olive oil, for frying

12–16 slices of French bread

4 garlic cloves, squashed, not peeled

125 ml rouille*

100 g grated Gruyère cheese

kitchen string

SERVES 6–8

Scrub and debeard the mussels. Tap them all against the work surface and discard any that don't close – they are dead – and any with damaged shells.

Heat 2 tablespoons olive oil in a very large, high-sided, saucepan. Add the mussels, garlic and wine. Cover the pan and shake over moderate heat for 4–6 minutes or until all the mussels have opened (discard any that remain closed).

Remove the pan from the heat and tip the contents into a colander lined with wet muslin or kitchen paper, set over a bowl to catch the juices. Remove and discard the shells from half the mussels. Set all the mussels aside and return the strained liquid to the pan. Tie the parsley and thyme into a bundle with string, then add to the pan, together with the cayenne and water or stock.

Put a pinch of saffron in the pan and crush the remainder with 2 teaspoons sea salt using a mortar and pestle. Add a splash of liquid to dissolve the powder, then add it to the pan.

Add the fennel, tomatoes and the fish to the pan and bring back to the boil. Reduce the heat and simmer, part-covered, for 6–8 minutes or until the fish is fairly well cooked. Add the squid and reserved mussels and cover the pan again just long enough to reheat the mussels and cook the squid until firm but not rubbery. Uncover the pan, sprinkle with Pernod, if using, and set aside while you make the croûtes.

Heat a little olive oil in a frying pan. Add the bread and fry on both sides until golden. Rub with the garlic cloves and top with the rouille and cheese.

To serve, put the croûtes in deep, heated soup plates, add a share of the fish, seafood and liquid and enjoy while the flavours, colours and aromas are at their best.

***Note** Rouille is available in cans and jars from large supermarkets.

mains

In this quick, pan-fried curry, the flavour comes mainly from chilli oil. As soon as the pan and oil are heated, add the clams, steam for just a few minutes and they're cooked.

baby clams
with chilli oil and holy basil

1 tablespoon peanut or sunflower oil

2 garlic cloves, finely chopped

1 kg fresh baby clams, in the shell

2 tablespoons Thai fish sauce

2 small fresh red chillies, thinly sliced

20 leaves holy basil

Chilli oil

2 tablespoons peanut or sunflower oil

4 tablespoons finely chopped garlic

4 tablespoons finely chopped shallots

4 tablespoons finely chopped dried red chillies

½ teaspoon sea salt

1 tablespoon sugar

SERVES 4

To make the chilli oil, heat the oil in a wok, add the garlic and stir-fry until golden brown. Remove the garlic with a fine sieve and set aside. Add the shallots to the wok and stir-fry until brown and crispy, then remove and set aside. Add the chillies to the wok and stir-fry until they begin to darken, then remove and set aside.

Using a mortar and pestle, pound the fried chillies, garlic and shallots together. Put the mixture back in the wok and stir over low heat. Stir in the salt and sugar and mix to make a thick, slightly oily reddish-black sauce, not a paste. You will need 1 tablespoon for this recipe, reserve the rest for another use.

To cook the clams, heat the peanut or sunflower oil in a large frying pan, add the garlic and fry until golden brown. Add 1 tablespoon of the chilli oil and the baby clams and stir well. Add the fish sauce, chillies and 4 tablespoons water. Stir thoroughly, add the basil, cover the pan and let steam for a few minutes until the clams have opened. Discard any that don't open. Stir again, transfer to warmed bowls and serve.

herb omelette with prawns

Iran (Persia) boasts one of the world's great cuisines, and this herb omelette (coucou sabzi) is one of its best-known dishes. Prawns have been added to make it a more substantial lunch dish. If you don't have a suitable oven dish, use a frying pan with an ovenproof handle to finish off the cooking. Fennel leaves can be hard to find in stores because they wilt easily. If you can't find them, use the green sprouting tops from bulb fennel instead.

To prepare the prawns, devein them, then 'butterfly' them – cut down the back lengthways, but leave the tail fins intact, so they will sit upright when cooked.

Put the eggs and milk in a bowl, add salt and pepper to taste and 2 tablespoons olive oil. Whisk briefly.

Put 2 tablespoons olive oil in a frying pan, heat gently, then add the chopped fennel and wilt for about 3 minutes. Add the spring onions and leek and stir to wilt a little. Stir into the egg mixture.

Put the leaves from the parsley, mint and oregano and half the fennel fronds on a board. Chop them all together, then stir into the eggs. Pour into the prepared ovenproof dish, then sit the prawns upright in the dish.

Cover carefully with foil and cook in a preheated oven at 180°C (350°F) Gas 4 for 25 minutes, then uncover and continue baking until cooked and golden, about 5 minutes more. Tear half the remaining fennel fronds over the top and set aside for a few minutes before serving.

Cut into wedges, including at least 1 prawn in each serving. Sprinkle with the remaining fennel fronds and serve with crusty bread and a crisp green salad.

6–8 uncooked prawns, shelled but with tail fins intact

6 large eggs

100 ml milk

5 tablespoons olive oil

1 small fennel bulb, thinly sliced, then chopped, and a large handful of the green leaves

3 spring onions, thinly sliced

1 young leek, thinly sliced

4 sprigs of fresh parsley

4 sprigs of fresh mint

a small handful of fresh oregano leaves

a large handful of fennel fronds

sea salt and freshly ground black pepper

To serve

crusty bread

crisp green salad

an ovenproof dish, 20 x 27 cm, preferably non-stick, oiled

SERVES 6

african seafood kebabs
with piri piri basting oil

The piri piri is a variety of fiercely hot chilli introduced to Africa by the Portuguese, probably via Western India. The name is also used for the hot sauces in which the pods are used. Versions of piri piri sauce can be found in many former Portuguese colonies, from Mozambique and Angola to Brazil, as well as Portugal itself.

12 large uncooked prawns, shelled but with tail fins intact

8 or 12 small scallops, trimmed

12–20 fresh bay leaves

ciabatta or focaccia bread, to serve

Piri piri basting oil

3 garlic cloves, crushed

5–6 red bird's eye chillies or 8–9 regular red chillies, deseeded and coarsely chopped

freshly squeezed juice of ½ lemon

100 ml extra virgin olive oil

½ teaspoon nigella seeds (optional)

4 metal skewers

SERVES 4

To make the piri piri basting oil, put the garlic, chillies, lemon juice and olive oil in a blender and process until smooth. Transfer to a bowl and stir in the nigella seeds, if using.

Dip the prawns and scallops in the basting oil and coat well. Thread the prawns and scallops alternately onto the skewers, with the bay leaves between them.

Set the skewers apart on a grill rack over a grill tray. Cook under a preheated hot grill for about 5 minutes, basting frequently with the piri piri oil and turning once halfway through, until the prawns and scallops are cooked. (Don't overcook the kebabs or the scallops will be tough – prawns and scallops are done when the flesh becomes opaque.) Alternatively, instead of basting the kebabs during grilling, put the basting oil in a small saucepan, boil for 1–2 minutes, then serve as a dipping sauce for the kebabs. Serve the kebabs with the bread.

2 tablespoons peanut or
sunflower oil

2 garlic cloves, finely chopped

12 uncooked king prawns,
shelled and deveined

600 ml coconut cream

600 ml vegetable stock

2 large fresh red chillies,
sliced diagonally into thin ovals

4 tablespoons Thai fish sauce

8 round green Thai
aubergines, quartered

1 tablespoon sugar

30 fresh Thai sweet basil leaves

Green curry paste

1 teaspoon coriander seeds

1 teaspoon cumin seeds

1 teaspoon white peppercorns

1 tablespoon chopped lemongrass

3 cm piece of fresh galangal or
ginger, peeled and chopped

2 long green chillies, chopped

10 small green chillies, chopped

2 tablespoons chopped garlic

3 Thai pink shallots or
2 regular ones, chopped

3 coriander roots, chopped

1 teaspoon finely chopped kaffir
lime leaves

2 teaspoons shrimp paste

SERVES 4

Green curry is a classic dish from Thailand. You can buy ready-made green curry paste from most supermarkets, but this homemade version is wonderful and well worth the effort.

green curry
with prawns

To make the green curry paste, put all the paste ingredients in a mortar and grind to a thick paste with a pestle.

Heat the oil in a large saucepan, add the garlic and fry until golden brown. Stir in 2 tablespoons curry paste, mixing well. Add the prawns and stir-fry until just cooked through, about 1 minute. Add the coconut cream and bring to the boil, stirring constantly. Add the vegetable stock and return to the boil, stirring constantly.

Keeping the curry simmering, add the chillies, fish sauce, aubergines and sugar and simmer until the aubergines are cooked but still crunchy (do not overcook or the prawns will be tough).

Stir in the basil leaves just before pouring into serving bowls. Serve with rice and other Thai dishes.

Cheese shortcrust pastry

225 g plain flour, plus extra for dusting

1 teaspoon salt

3 tablespoons freshly grated Parmesan cheese

125 g unsalted butter, chilled and diced

2 egg yolks

2–3 tablespoons iced water

Chilli crab filling

2 tablespoons olive oil

a bunch of spring onions, sliced

6 eggs

300 ml double cream

1 tablespoon Dijon mustard

500 g fresh or frozen white crab meat, thawed and drained

8 mild, sweet pickled red chillies, deseeded and roughly chopped

100 g freshly grated Parmesan cheese

freshly ground black pepper

a loose-based tart tin, 25 cm diameter, 3 cm deep

foil or baking parchment and baking beans

a baking sheet

SERVES 6–8

crab and sweet pickled chilli tart

The sweet and salty taste of fresh crab (if you can get it) mixed with mild red chillies pickled in sweet vinegar is fantastic. They seem made for each other. Serve this with an avocado salsa or just plain sliced avocado dressed with a coriander vinaigrette.

To make the pastry, sift the flour and salt into a bowl. Stir in the Parmesan, then rub in the butter using the tips of your fingers. Mix the egg yolks with 2 tablespoons iced water, then stir into the flour mixture to bind to a firm but malleable dough (if it is too dry, stir in another tablespoon of water). Knead lightly until smooth, then shape into a flattened ball. Wrap in clingfilm and chill for at least 30 minutes.

Bring the pastry to room temperature. On a lightly floured work surface, roll the pastry out to a thickness of 3 mm and use to line the tart tin. Prick the base all over with a fork, then chill or freeze for 15 minutes.

Line the pastry case with foil or baking parchment, then fill with baking beans. Set on a baking sheet and bake blind in the centre of a preheated oven at 200°C (400°F) Gas 6 for 10–12 minutes. Remove the foil or baking parchment and baking beans and return the pastry case to the oven for 5–7 minutes more to dry out completely. Remove from the oven and let cool. Reduce the oven temperature to 180°C (350°F) Gas 4.

To make the filling, heat the olive oil in a frying pan, add the spring onions and fry until softened, but not coloured. Let cool slightly. Put the eggs, cream and mustard in a bowl and whisk well. Stir in the crab, cooked spring onions, sweet chillies and Parmesan, then season with plenty of black pepper. Spoon into the pastry case and level the surface. Set on a baking sheet and bake for about 45 minutes until just firm.

Serve warm or at room temperature.

pasta & rice

seafood spaghettini

Vary the seafood depending on what's available and best on the day, but always include clams or mussels – for their flavour as well as their beautiful shells.

500 g fresh mussels or clams, in the shell

300 g dried pasta, such as spaghettini

4–5 tablespoons olive oil

300 g mixed seafood, such as squid, cut into rings, shelled prawns and scallops, halved crossways

2 tablespoons chopped fresh flat leaf parsley

sea salt and freshly ground black pepper

SERVES 4

Scrub and debeard the mussels, if using. Tap the mussels or clams against the work surface and discard any that don't close – they are dead – and any with damaged shells.

Bring a large saucepan of water to the boil. Add a good pinch of salt, then the pasta, and cook until *al dente*, or according to the timings on the packet.

Meanwhile, heat half the oil in a large sauté pan or saucepan. Add the mixed seafood and cook for 3–4 minutes, stirring constantly until just cooked. Transfer to a large bowl and set aside.

Add the mussels or clams to the seafood pan, cover with a lid and cook for about 5 minutes until all the shells have opened, discarding any that remain closed.

Drain the pasta well and return it to the warm pan. Add the mussels or clams, mixed seafood, parsley and the remaining olive oil. Add salt and pepper to taste, toss gently to mix, then serve immediately.

A delicious, low fat pasta dish? Yes it's true.
Better still, it's ready to serve in 15 minutes.

mussels in white wine
with linguine

1 kg fresh mussels, in the shell

300 g dried pasta, such as linguine or tagliatelle

150 ml dry white wine

2 garlic cloves, finely chopped

1 fresh red chilli, deseeded and finely chopped

2 tablespoons chopped fresh flat leaf parsley

sea salt and freshly ground black pepper

olive oil, to serve

SERVES 4

Scrub and debeard the mussels. Tap them all against the work surface and discard any that don't close – they are dead – and any with damaged shells.

Bring a large saucepan of water to the boil. Add a good pinch of salt, then the pasta, and cook until *al dente*, or according to the timings on the packet.

Meanwhile, put the wine, garlic and chilli in another large saucepan, bring to the boil and simmer rapidly for 5 minutes. Season with freshly ground black pepper. Add the mussels, cover with a lid and cook for 5 minutes, shaking the pan from time to time, until all the shells have opened. Discard any that remain closed.

Drain the pasta and return it to the warm pan. Add the parsley and mussels and toss gently to mix. Divide among 4 bowls, sprinkle with olive oil and serve immediately.

pappardelle
with seafood sauce

Home-made pasta is not as difficult as you might think, and pappardelle is easier to make than most. Olive oil is the perfect vehicle for sauces and marries well with elegant ingredients such as lobster, prawns or crab. It makes pasta a special-occasion dish.

To make the pappardelle, put the flour, eggs and 2 teaspoons sea salt flakes in a food processor. Work in bursts for 1 minute until the mixture comes together in a crumbly mass, then into a rough ball. Knead it firmly together, then transfer to a floured work surface. Knead for 2 minutes, then wrap in clingfilm and chill for 1 hour.

Divide the dough into 4 parts, keeping 3 still wrapped. Starting on the thickest setting of the pasta machine, roll 1 piece of dough through 3–4 times, folding the 2 ends into the middle each time to get a plump envelope of dough and giving it a half turn each time. Lightly flour the dough on both sides.

Roll it through all the settings on the pasta machine, starting at the thickest, about 6 times in all, until you get a 1 metre length of pasta (cut it in half if it's easier). Hang this over a chair or pole to air-dry. Repeat with the 3 remaining balls of dough. Roll up each length, then slice into 2.5 cm wide ribbons. Unroll, dust in semolina flour, then cut each in half, to make strips about 50 cm long.

To make the sauce, heat the oil in a heavy-based frying pan. Add the lobster, prawns or crab meat, dill, chives, 1 tablespoon lemon juice, salt and pepper. Heat briefly until the flavours blend, then keep warm over very low heat.

Bring a large saucepan of water to the boil. Add a pinch of salt, then the pasta and cook for 1½ minutes. Drain the pasta, then tip it into the sauce. Toss gently with 2 wooden spoons, add the lemon zest and serve immediately in warmed pasta bowls.

180 ml extra virgin olive oil

450 g lobster meat, from 1 kg whole lobster, or prawns or crab meat

1 bunch of dill, chopped

1 bunch of chives, chopped

shredded zest and juice of 1 unwaxed lemon

sea salt and freshly crushed black pepper

Pappardelle

500 g tipo 00 flour*, plus extra for dusting

5 free-range eggs

2 teaspoons sea salt flakes, crushed

semolina flour, for dusting

a pasta machine

SERVES 4

* Use this special Italian fine-grade flour (available from Italian delicatessens) to make your own pasta. If utterly unobtainable, use plain flour instead. Alternatively, use dried pasta.

seafood with couscous

1.5 kg assorted non-oily fish and shellfish, such as monkfish, red snapper, crayfish, lobster, crabs, prawns, mussels and clams

1 teaspoon sea salt

4 garlic cloves, sliced

4 celery stalks, sliced

1 head of fennel, quartered

20 black peppercorns, crushed

30 cm strip of unwaxed orange zest

30 cm strip of unwaxed lemon zest

a large bunch of wild oregano or thyme, fresh or dried

1–2 tablespoons tomato purée

Cuscusu

500 g coarse 'instant' couscous

1 onion, sliced

2 green chillies, thinly sliced

2 tablespoons extra virgin olive oil

750 ml boiling seafood stock or hot water

1 teaspoon orange flower water (optional)

freshly squeezed juice of 1 orange

sea salt and freshly ground black pepper

SERVES 4–6

In this delicious recipe, originally from Trapani in Sicily, a generous fish stew is ladled over the aromatic cuscusu *and the juices add their flavour to its fragrant charms. Modern 'instant' or precooked couscous is quick and easy because it needs only moistening and heating – a bonus, because cooking traditional North African couscous requires skill and is very time-consuming.*

If using fresh mussels, scrub and debeard them. Tap all mussels and clams against the work surface and discard any that don't close – they are dead – and any with damaged shells.

Cut the fish and shellfish into 3 cm chunks or, if small, leave whole. Put in a very large flameproof casserole, add the salt, garlic, celery, fennel, peppercorns and 500 ml water and bring to the boil. Stir in the orange and lemon zest, oregano or thyme, and enough tomato purée to make the liquid rosy. Reduce the heat to simmering. Cover and cook for 10 minutes.

To prepare the *cuscusu*, put the couscous, onion, chillies, olive oil, salt and pepper in a heatproof bowl. Pour in the boiling stock or water. Stir and leave for 5 minutes to plump up. Stir in the orange flower water. When all the liquid has been absorbed, add the orange juice.

Put the *cuscusu* in deep serving bowls and spoon the fish and its broth over the top and serve.

You can make this with fresh or frozen prepared squid. If you have the tentacles, they make a great topping – just quickly sear them on a stove-top grill pan. You could fry a little extra sliced garlic and some chopped red chilli in olive oil and pour this over the risotto before serving, if you like.

squid risotto

300 g squid, fresh or
frozen and thawed

about 1.5 litres hot chicken
stock or vegetable stock

125 g unsalted butter

1 onion or 2 shallots,
finely chopped

2–3 large garlic cloves,
finely chopped

75 ml dry white wine

300 g risotto rice,
preferably carnaroli

2 tablespoons chopped
fresh parsley

1–2 tablespoons olive oil

sea salt and freshly ground
black pepper

a stove-top grill pan (optional)

SERVES 4

To prepare the squid, see page 21. Cut the squid into rings or small pieces and reserve the tentacles, if using.

Put the stock in a saucepan and keep at a gentle simmer. Melt half the butter in a large, heavy saucepan, then add the onion or shallots and the garlic. Cook gently for 5 minutes until translucent but not browned. Add the squid, then the wine and cook gently for 5 minutes until the squid is white and the wine beginning to disappear. Add the rice and stir until well coated with the butter, wine and squid and heated through.

Begin adding the stock, a large ladle at a time, stirring gently until each ladle has almost been absorbed by the rice. The risotto should be kept at a bare simmer throughout cooking, so don't let the rice dry out – add more stock as necessary. Continue until the rice is tender and creamy, but the grains still firm. (This should take 15–20 minutes depending on the type of rice used – check the packet instructions.)

Taste and season well with salt and pepper and beat in the remaining butter and the parsley. Cover and let rest for a couple of minutes.

Meanwhile, heat a stove-top grill pan to smoking hot, toss the tentacles, if using, in the olive oil to coat, then add them to the pan. Cook for 1–2 minutes, then remove to a plate. Check the risotto – you may like to add a little more hot stock just before you serve to loosen it, but don't let it wait around too long or the rice will turn mushy. Serve with the tentacles on top.

index

African seafood kebabs, 49

beansprouts: laksa lemak, 36
bouillabaisse, 43

char-grilled scallop salad, 33
chillies: baby clams with chilli oil and holy
    basil, 45
    crab and sweet pickled chilli tart, 53
    green curry with prawns, 50
    piri piri basting oil, 49
    Thai lobster noodle soup, 39
chowder, clam, 40
clams: baby clams with chilli oil and holy basil, 45
    clam chowder, 40
    Spanish clams with ham, 14
couscous, seafood with, 61
crab: crab and sweet pickled chilli tart, 53
    spicy crab in filo cups, 10
crayfish party, Swedish, 29
croûtes, 43
curries: baby clams with chilli oil and holy
    basil, 45
    green curry with prawns, 50

eggs: herb omelette with prawns, 46

fennel: herb omelette with prawns, 46
filo cups, spicy crab in, 10

Greek octopus salad, 30
green curry with prawns, 50

ham, Spanish clams with, 14
herb omelette with prawns, 46
hot and sour soup with prawns, 35

kebabs, African seafood, 49

laksa lemak, 36
lemon, sizzled scallops with, 17
lobster: pappardelle with seafood sauce, 58
    Thai lobster noodle soup, 39

mayonnaise, squid with, 18
mussels: baked mussels with crispy
    breadcrumbs, 13
    bouillabaisse, 43
    mussels in ice wine, 25
    mussels in white wine with linguine, 57
    seafood spaghettini, 55

noodles: laksa lemak, 36
    Thai lobster noodle soup, 39

octopus: Greek octopus salad, 30
    marinated octopus, 22
omelettes: herb omelette with prawns, 46

pancetta: char-grilled scallop salad, 33
    clam chowder, 40
pappardelle with seafood sauce, 58
pasta: mussels in white wine with linguine, 57
    pappardelle with seafood sauce, 58
    seafood spaghettini, 55
peas: char-grilled scallop salad, 33
piri piri basting oil, 49
potatoes: clam chowder, 40
prawns: African seafood kebabs, 49
    green curry with prawns, 50
    herb omelette with prawns, 46
    hot and sour soup with prawns, 35
    laksa lemak, 36
    prawns in overcoats, 9
    spicy Thai prawn salad, 26

risotto, squid, 62

salads: char-grilled scallop salad, 33
    Greek octopus salad, 30
    spicy Thai prawn salad, 26
scallops: African seafood kebabs, 49
    char-grilled scallop salad, 33
    sizzled scallops with lemon, 17
seafood spaghettini, 55
seafood with couscous, 61
snacks, 8–23
soups, 34–43
    bouillabaisse, 43
    clam chowder, 40
    hot and sour soup with prawns, 35
    laksa lemak, 36
    Thai lobster noodle soup, 39
Spanish clams with ham, 14
squid: bouillabaisse, 43
    oven-roasted baby squid, 21
    squid risotto, 62
    squid with mayonnaise, 18
Swedish crayfish party, 29

tart, crab and sweet pickled chilli, 53
Thai lobster noodle soup, 39
Thai prawn salad, 26

wine: bouillabaisse, 43
    mussels in ice wine, 25

recipe credits

Julz Beresford
Pages 9, 22

Vatcharin Bhumichitr
Pages 35, 45, 50

Maxine Clark
Pages 10, 13, 53, 62

Clare Ferguson
Pages 14, 17, 18, 21, 43, 58, 61

Silvana Franco
Pages 55, 57

Manisha Gambhir Harkins
Pages 36, 49

Elsa Petersen-Schepelern
Pages 25, 26, 29, 30, 33, 40

Linda Tubby
Pages 39, 46

photography credits

Martin Brigdale
Pages 2, 3, 7, 11, 12, 15, 19, 25, 52,
60, 63

Peter Cassidy
Pages 8–9, 16, 20, 23, 24–25, 27,
28, 31, 32, 34–35, 37, 38, 41, 42,
44–45, 45, 47, 48, 51, 55, 59

William Lingwood
Pages 1, 4–5, 36, 54–55, 56

David Montgomery
Page 9

Ian Wallace
Page 6